STUDY GUIDE

UTTERLY AMAZED

STORIES FROM OUTSIDE THE BOAT

JOHN ANDREWS

CONTENTS

PREFACE

WE BEGAN PRAYING A three-fold prayer before *Utterly Amazed* was even released. We asked God to help us:

- point people to Jesus who don't know Him
- brag on Jesus by telling His stories.
- encourage and empower Believers to step out of their boat and trust Jesus to do something "crazy" in and through them.

Nobel Prize Winner, John R. Mott once said, "The one who does the work is only surpassed in value by the one who multiplies the doers."

That is the purpose of this small group study…

- For God to personalize for you the spiritual need across this planet for Him.
- For God to show you *your part* in meeting that need.
- To multiply the numbers of those willing to step out of their own boat to grow the Kingdom.
- And for you to see how He has *already* equipped you for the task He has for you.

You can walk through this Study Guide on your own or with a group. Obviously, if you are doing this study alone, please do so at your own pace, and let God speak in His time. We would love to hear from you after you finish. There is contact information in the back of this guide to show you how to tell us your story.

If you are walking through this with a small group, Sunday School class, FCA Huddle, college group or even with your entire church, we recommend using it as a 10-week study, reading corresponding chapters in both the book and the Study Guide each week. Then come back together to discuss what you've read and answered over the course of the previous week.

Week 1 is designed for the leader/facilitator to cast the vision for the study and to make sure everyone has a book and a Study Guide. We want your group to be able to read through the Introduction and Chapter 1 in order to be prepared for Week 2. Starting Week 1, even before anyone has been able to do any reading, we want to help you and your group begin this journey. We have resources for group leaders to help kickstart this study, including group dis-cussion questions for Week 1 at www.UtterlyAmazed.com/resources-guides.

Here is a proposed outline for you to follow.

Proposed Study Guide Outline for Small Groups

- Week 1: Course Introduction/Vision Casting

- Week 2: Introduction and Chapter 1

- Week 3: Chapter 2 and Chapter 3

- Week 4: Chapter 4 and Chapter 5

- Week 5: Chapter 6, Chapter 7, and Chapter 8

- Week 6: Chapter 9 and Chapter 10

- Week 7: Chapter 11 and Chapter 12

- Week 8: Chapter 13 and Chapter 14

- Week 9: Chapter 15, Chapter 16, and Chapter 17

- Week 10: Chapter 18 and Conclusion

INTRODUCTION

READ MATTHEW 14:25-31. As you read, it's important to note the disciples didn't have the luxury of Scripture like we do. It would be easy for us today to look at this story and say, "Of course, Jesus could walk on water!" Or, "Why shouldn't Peter ask Jesus to call him out?" We've heard this story before, but for the disciples, it was a daily adventure with Jesus, always learning something new about His power and sovereignty.

BUT…the sea and the storm themselves were not new! At least four professional fishermen who had grown up on the Sea of Galilee were in the boat. They knew what they were up against and how serious this was, including the one asking to get out of the boat! Everyone in the boat with Peter thought what he was asking was crazy--some of them probably even told him so. But he didn't care. *He was so focused on Jesus and what He could do through Him, that what everyone else was saying didn't matter.*

Think about a time where you were so focused on doing something that the naysayers didn't have any effect on you? Note: It could have been a great thing, or a really bad decision! Write it here.

_____

_____

_____

_____

What about the opposite? Have you ever had something you knew God was moving you toward, but you let the negative voices around you distract you from that purpose? What was it?

_____

_____

_____

_____

_____

> Flee the evil desires of youth and pursue
> righteousness, faith, love and peace, along with
> those who call on the Lord out of a pure heart.
>
> *II Timothy 2:22 (NIV)*

Why do you think it's so important to *pursue* righteousness and not just *flee* temptation?

_____

_____

_____

_____

_____

A study was done about 10 years ago testing the theory that we have a natural draw/lean to our dominant side. This theory was tested on a football field. Test subjects would start in the back corner of one end of the field facing the opposite end. Right-handed subjects started on the left side, while left-handed subjects started on the right side. After being blindfolded, each subject was instructed to walk in a straight line to the other end of the field.

In almost every account, while walking, the subject drifted toward their dominant side across the field and out of bounds on the far side before they ever made it to the other end of the field!

The point is, whether fleeing a good or bad situation, left to drift on our own without any direction we will eventually end up right back where we started. Sound familiar? How has that happened to you?

To find direction, we can't just *flee*. We must *pursue*. Take the blindfold off and chase after Him. No one had a problem staying on their initial sideline if they weren't blindfolded, when they knew where they were going, what they were chasing.

Peter did what no other man had ever done. Jesus did the impossible through Peter, but Peter's trust, obedience and courage were required first! What is that "crazy" something you know that God is calling you to, but you've not yet been willing to obey? Write it down now, so maybe, just maybe, when you finish this journey you can come back and scratch it out!

Look at the nations and watch and be utterly amazed, for I am going to do something in your days that you would not believe, even if you were told.

Habakkuk 1:1-5 (NIV)

The Prophet Habakkuk was complaining about evil people succeeding and going unpunished. In this context, God's response in verse 5 above was referring to the people of Israel and their enemies but it's also true for us today. God is telling us He stands ready to do something in and through us that is so far-fetched, so hard to believe, if He told us before He did it we could only say "No, God, you're crazy!"

As the Body of Christ, do we believe God can and will do something amazing and unbelievable in us? Do *you* believe so? Are you praying for that? Do you even want it to happen? If so, write it down.

_____

_____

_____

_____

_____

_____

What does "operating in the crazy" (page x) look like for you?

_____

_____

_____

_____

Have you ever asked God to personalize the Great Commission for you? What would happen if you did?

_____

_____

_____

_____

Look at Matthew 28:18-20 (NLT):

> Jesus came and told his disciples, "I have been given all authority in heaven and on earth. Therefore, go and make disciples of all the nations, baptizing them in the name of the Father and the Son and the Holy Spirit. Teach these new disciples to obey all the commands I have given you. And be sure of this: I am with you always, even to the end of the age."

The original Greek word for "go" actually means "as you are going." Read the passage above again, substituting those words. You may never travel to another nation personally, but each of us, wherever we are, should be affected by those four words, "as you are going." How does that change your view on going "to the nations?"

The Greek word for "nations" here is *ethos,* the origin of our word "ethnic." Therefore, Jesus isn't just calling us to the political entities which we call nations. Jesus is calling us to every people group and ethnicity, no matter how near or far away they might be. How does substituting "people group/ethnicity" for "nations" in the Great Commission change your mindset on missions?

_____

_____

_____

_____

Missions just mean more when we are able to put a face and a name to those we are serving. When we "know" them, the connection is stronger and more significant. Think of being a fan at an athletic contest. It doesn't matter if it's Saturday morning recreation basketball or the NBA, kids' flag football or the NFL, when you personally know someone competing, it just means more. The same is true for missions. If you were able to *know* someone who doesn't even know about Jesus because they live in a restricted, foreign setting. How would it change your outlook on Missions?

_____

_____

_____

Your eyes saw my unformed body; all the days
ordained for me were written in your book
before one of them came to be.

Psalm 139:16 (NLT)

Think about that for a moment: before every day in your life, every moment - both good and bad, every win or loss, every wise and unwise decision you've ever made, every success and every failure even happened, He had written them down in His book, before even one had happened! How does it make you feel, knowing that God designed the Great Commission so personally?

_____

_____

_____

_____

Most importantly, we all have different things that make us comfortable. Before we really begin this journey together…what is the comfort zone you know God is asking you to leave behind for what He has for you next? In other words, what is your *boat*?

_____

_____

_____

The Great Commission is not a suggestion, it is a commandment. Author and speaker, Francis Chan is well known for having said on multiple occasions, "Simon says, 'pat your head' and we pat our heads. Jesus says 'go and make disciples' and we memorize the verse."

What is *your* next step toward getting out of *your* boat?

_____

_____

_____

_____

_____

_____

_____

_____

_____

_____

CHAPTER 1

FOR GENERATIONS

WE ARE CONSUMED BY a culture focused on self-promotion, self-interest, and self- preservation. However, if we're honest, we long to feel small, to know there is something out there bigger than we are that will ultimately take care of us or protect us.

Read Job 38:8-11 (NLT):

> Who kept the sea inside its boundaries as it burst
> from the womb, and as I clothed it with clouds
> and wrapped it in thick darkness? For I locked
> it behind barred gates, limiting its shores. I said,
> "This far and no farther will you come. Here
> your proud waves must stop!"

God told ALL the waves on EVERY beach on the planet where to stop! How can a God who tells the waves where to stop, help you in your day to day? Can He redeem your past? Can you trust Him with your future? Thoughts? Write them down here.

_____

_____

_____

_____

We've seen people all over the world searching...to know there is something out there, for whom they have been created to worship. Why do we all search/long to know there is something greater than ourselves?

_____

_____

_____

_____

_____

Read Romans 1:18-20 (NIV):

> The wrath of God is being revealed from heaven
> against all the godlessness and wickedness
> of people, who suppress the truth by their
> wickedness, since what may be known about
> God is plain to them, because God has made it
> plain to them. For since the creation of the world
> God's invisible qualities—his eternal power and
> divine nature—have been clearly seen, being
> understood from what has been made, so that
> people are without excuse.

Do you really believe God would condemn those that have never heard about Him? Why would a loving God do that?

_____

_____

_____

_____

_____

_____

How does Romans 1:18-20 affect your heart on global missions and the billions that are lost?

_____

_____

_____

Look at these stats from thetravelingteam.org:
- Over 3 Billion people on the planet have never heard the name of Jesus…not even once!
- Over 4 Billion have no access to the Gospel!
- Of the 400,000 cross-cultural missionaries working worldwide, only **three percent** go to the unreached!
- Only $1 of every $100,000 that Christians earn is going to reach the unreached, which is 42.5% of the world!
- 60% of unreached people groups live in countries closed to missionaries from North America.
- 1.51 billion people, speaking 6,661 languages, do not have a full Bible in their first language.
- There are over 900,000 international students in the U.S each year. 80% of those students will return to their countries having never been invited into an American home!
- 30:1…Roughly thirty-times as many missionaries go to Reached People Groups to work with Christians, as go to the Unreached People Groups! Far less than that go to the Frontier People Groups (no more than one Christian per 1,000 individuals).

How do these statistics impact your perspective on the global need?

On our first "official" mission trip 17 years ago, we went to a 95% Buddhist country in SE Asia. A few nights into the trip, my wife began to cry in our hotel room. Not knowing why, I asked her what she was feeling.

Through her tears, she said, "I don't understand why God would do this. I don't understand why we've been so blessed to be saturated with the Gospel our entire lives, and these people have never even heard the Gospel once!"

I didn't have an answer. We just sat there, overwhelmed at the lostness all around us. A few nights later she said with no tears, but with no less intensity, "I've figured it out. I know why God blessed us and tasked us with the Gospel. If these folks had the Gospel and we didn't, there'd be no way they could get to us, they don't have the same resources that we have!"

Here are two hypothetical statistics released by thetravelingteam.org.

- "Evangelical Christians could provide all of the funds needed to plant a church in each of the 7,400 unreached people groups with only 0.03% of their income!"
- "The Church has roughly 3,000 times the financial resources and 9,000 times the manpower needed to finish the Great Commission. If every evangelical Christian gave 10% of their income to missions we could easily support 2 million new missionaries."

It's very easy to say "The task is too big, too great. I can't do anything about it." That is just not true. What can you be doing now, to prepare for what God has for your future? What can you do today?

_____

_____

_____

Read the words of Jesus in John 6:44a (NIV):

"For no one can come to me unless the Father who sent me draws them to me..."

How could the Chief and his Elders surrender their lives to Jesus right there in the courtyard of their village only a few minutes after hearing the Gospel for the first time as we read on page 11?

_____

_____

They knew they needed to be worshiping something. They just didn't know what until they found Him that day (p.13). There are still billions on this earth just like the Chief. What will you do about it?

_____

_____

CHAPTER 2

I HAVE NO PEACE

Each time He said, "My grace is all you need.
My power works best in weakness." So now I
am glad to boast about my weaknesses, so that
the power of Christ can work through me.

II Corinthians 12:9 (NLT)

How does reading God's words to Paul make you feel about God's power? How have you seen God's power show up in your weakness?

_____

_____

_____

_____

_____

_____

_____

_____

_____

_____

Trust in the LORD with all your heart and lean not on your own understanding; in all your ways submit to Him, and He will make your paths straight.

Proverbs 3:5-6 (NIV)

I had to come to terms with God's plan for my life on my flight over to the Middle East (p.17), and God settled my heart with the words from Hebrews 13:6 (NIV).

> So we say with confidence, "The Lord is my helper; I will not be afraid. What can mere mortals do to me?"

Do you *really* trust HIM with your life? Have you come to accept His plan for your life, regardless of how much of that plan you may or may not know right now? How will that affect your future? Your family's future?

_____

_____

_____

_____

How has that trust changed the way you live your life today?

_____

_____

_____

_____

_____

On one of our trips to the Middle East, a young man named Ali, said, "*We believe that Allah has 99 different names, so all those strings of beads either have 11, 33, or 99 beads on them. So, in times when we are nervous, or have a reason to call on Allah, we are supposed to thumb through those beads, and call out a different name on each bead. Reminding ourselves of those different names is supposed to help us know Allah more*" (p.25-26).

Did you know God also has many names? He only gives himself two names in Scripture, "Yahweh" and "I am" found in Exodus 3. The Bible authors present us with many more throughout the Word. List as many names and meanings as you know.

_____

_____

_____

_____

_____

_____

_____

When the prophet Isaiah prophesied about the coming Son of God in Isaiah 9:6 (NIV), he gave several names for God. "For to us a child is born, to us a son is given, and the government will be on his shoulders. And He will be called Wonderful Counselor, Mighty God, Everlasting Father, **Prince of Peace**."

Ali believed that he would go to heaven after he died only if at the end of his life, his good outweighed his bad. That belief is very common among religions around the world, but it is ALSO very common here. Ali said he "had no peace" and thought it was because he and his family could be killed at any time. Then I said, *"Forget being fearful of 'The Bad Guys', not knowing the answer to that question would give me no peace."*

*"You're right. I've never thought about that before. I've always thought my lack of peace was because of all that was happening around me, and the uncertainty that surrounded me and my loved ones every day. I think it may simply be because **I'll never know if I'm good enough.**" (p.29)*

You CAN know you are good enough...*"Jesus is my Prince of Peace. I know you may not understand this, but I know I'm good enough. I know what will happen to me when I die. Jesus died in my place. He took my worthlessness and my faults and all the bad on my scale and put it on his own shoulders, on his scale. Then, because He really is the Son of God, and was the only perfect person to live on this earth, when He died for me, He paid my sin debt, and now God looks at me as righteous and holy though I am anything but."* (p. 30)

How do we know that we are good enough? Paul tells us in II Corinthians 5:21(NIV):

> God made him who had no sin to be sin
> for us, so that in him we might become the
> *righteousness* of God.

Do you *believe* that you are the righteousness of God? How does your life show it?

_____

_____

_____

_____

The enemy uses shame and guilt to try and keep us right where Ali was. Take a minute. Get away. Be quiet. Pray this directly to the Father...

"Thank you for paying my sin debt, a price/penalty that I could NEVER pay myself. I know that your Word promises that I am the "righteousness of God." Help me move past the shame and guilt of past mistakes and live in the freedom and peace that comes from knowing that truth, so that I can then help others do the same."

Write down any thoughts or feelings you may have after praying that prayer and spending some quiet time with God.

_____

_____

_____

_____

_____

CHAPTER 3

I WANT TO HAVE THAT LIGHT

THIS STORY TAKES PLACE in East Asia where we simply go to city parks and/or university campuses and "just show up and play." Very simple. Very easy. No specific protocol to follow, but we would have never seen God do the things He did on these trips if we didn't "just show up and play." It doesn't matter if you're a husband, wife, son or daughter, co-worker, teammate, etc. People around you need you to "just show up and play everyday." "Playing" may look different for different people, but we all have something to *play*.

Read King David's words:

> Praise the Lord with melodies on the lyre;
> make music for Him on the ten-stringed harp,
> Sing a new song of praise to Him;
> *play skillfully* on the harp, and sing with joy.

Psalm 33:2-3 (NLT)

David is not saying that if you can't play the harp or lyre, you have nothing to do. What he is saying is that we all have an "instrument" to play for God's glory, and it is up to us to work at and develop that skill. What is your "instrument?" Maybe you've never thought about that before. Take a few minutes and list a few possible "instruments" that God has given you to play for His glory.

_____

_____

_____

Where in your life are people counting on you to simply "show up and play?"

_____

_____

_____

_____

What might happen if you were obedient and intentional in using your "instrument" for His Glory?

_____

_____

_____

_____

On p. 36, I talk about being present when Q had his "light bulb" moment, when he realized God had a purpose and plan for his life. Do you believe God has a purpose AND plan for your life? If so, what is it? Write it down.

_____

_____

_____

_____

_____

For we are God's handiwork, created in Christ Jesus to do good works, which God prepared in advance for us to do.

Ephesians 2:10 (NIV)

Think about that for a moment. You are God's "handiwork." He made you exactly the way He wanted to, for the purpose He has for your life. Different translations substitute other words for "handiwork:" *craftsmanship, masterpiece, creative work*, and even *poetry.*

Each of those require attention to detail, time and intentionality. God was deliberate and intentional when He made you. Is it *possible* that God's plan for you may be bigger than you ever thought? How does this change your outlook on your future?

_____

_____

_____

_____

_____

_____

He fashioned you to fulfill a role only meant for you! Looking at the end of Ephesians 2:10, we see He prepared in advance the good works that we are to do. Now look at Psalm 139:16 (NLT):

> You saw me before I was born. Every day of my life was recorded in your book. Every moment was laid out *before a single had passed.*

Let that sink in for a minute. God recorded every day of your life in His book before you lived even one of them! What does that mean about God's purpose for your life?

_____

_____

_____

_____

Read I Corinthians 12:7-14. Why did God give each of us spiritual gifts? Do you have an idea of your gifts and your purpose in using them? What are they? What does this passage say to you about how the Body of Christ should work together?

_____

_____

_____

_____

_____

If you are unsure about what spiritual gifts you may have, Lifeway offers a simple tool to help figure them out.

https://explorethebible.lifeway.com/wp-content/ uploads/2018/03/DOC-Spiritual-Gifts-Survey.pdf

When I asked Q (p. 42) what he had been reading in his new Bible, he pointed out Matthew 5:14-16 (NLT):

> You are the light of the world—like a city on a hilltop that cannot be hidden. No one lights a lamp and then puts it under a basket. Instead, a lamp is placed on a stand, where it gives light to everyone in the house. In the same way, let your good deeds shine out for all to see, so that everyone will praise your heavenly Father.

Q ultimately realized he could not be the *light of the world* until Christ lived in him. That is how we become the *light of the world*, by letting Him shine out of us. If Christ doesn't live in you, you cannot be the light. If you have never truly surrendered your life to Jesus, make today the day.

Consider this: whether you find yourself in some little-known place around the globe, a maximum-security prison, in a gym after a ball game, or in a pew in your church for 40 years, the message is still the same.

We all have sinned and fallen short of the standard that God has set for our lives. He requires perfection from us because He is Holy and perfect. He cannot look on sin, and there is nothing you can do in your own power to change that. That is where Jesus comes in. Because He paid the penalty for your sin and mine, and then defeated death by rising from the grave three days later, we can be made holy in God's sight by accepting Him as our Lord and Savior. If you want to give your life to Him today, simply pray something like this to Him from your heart. There is no magic in the words. Only God can save. He just wants you. He wants your heart and life.

Father, I know that I am a sinner. I know that
you created me to have a relationship with
you. I know there is nothing I can do in my own
power to make that happen. So, Jesus, I ask
you right now to come into my life, forgive me of
my sin that separates me from you, and the best
way that I know how, from this point forward,
I'm going to live for you. Thank you, Jesus, for
saving me. (p.187)

If you just gave your life to Jesus, tell someone! There
is strength that can be drawn from the Body of Christ.
You can begin to learn how to live your new life in Jesus.
That is the next step in becoming that *light*. Jesus now lives
inside of you, and when you no longer do the things you've
always done, people are going to want to know why. You
can then tell them, "Because I have Jesus living inside of me
now." That is you *having* the light of the world.

The final Biblical truth we see in Q's life is him taking
the next step in *being that light*. The first thing Q did was
to take his new found friends to his loved ones so they
could help him explain the decision he had just made, and
how they could make the same decision. It reminds me of
Andrew when he first encountered Jesus in John 1.

Andrew, Simon Peter's brother, was one of
these men who heard what John said and then
followed Jesus. Andrew went to find his brother,
Simon, and told him, "We have found the
Messiah" (which means "Christ"). Then Andrew
brought Simon to meet Jesus.

John 1:40-42 (NLT)

Just like both Q and Andrew, there are people in your life that you need to go get and "bring to Jesus." Think about who they are and list them below.

_____

_____

_____

_____

_____

_____

CHAPTER 4

LEAVE *HIS* MARK

IN THIS CHAPTER, **I** talked about seeing the Argentine Offensive Coordinator's playbook (p.51). It was the largest playbook I'd ever seen. He had never played or coached football, so how could he have accumulated such a detailed wealth of offensive football knowledge? When I asked, he very plainly told me that he had printed off all of the plays and their diagrams from the Madden video game! All of that knowledge really did him no good, because he had no real football experience. He was pretending to be something that he wasn't, and what's more, he didn't even realize there was no magic in those plays.

It got me thinking...how many times do we show up with our "elaborate playbook" in hand, but have no idea what we're doing? We're just pretending. In what parts of your life are you just pretending right now, hoping no one finds out who you really are?

_____

_____

_____

_____

_____

_____

_____

_____

There was a significant difference between that Offensive Coordinator and the coaches that had come with me. He knew *about* football. Our coaches *knew* football. It reminded me of the story in John 3 of Nicodemus coming to Jesus at night. Nicodemus was a Pharisee. Jesus clashed with the Pharisees more than any other group during His ministry. They were religious leaders. The amount of information they had learned and memorized was simply staggering, but it's easy to see with Nicodemus' encounter with Jesus, he *knew about* the things of God, but he didn't *know* God. Read John 3:1-17 and answer the following questions:

1. Why did Nicodemus come to Jesus at night?

2. What is the spiritual rebirth to which Jesus is referring here?

3. John 3:16 is the most famous and well-known verse in the entire Bible. "For God so loved the WORLD...." I have always considered this to be meant for the whole world, which it is. But when these words were first spoken, Jesus was meeting with one man, alone at

night so no one else would know. It was
personal. Jesus is personal. In fact, as He was
speaking these words to Nicodemus, Jesus
may have even said it this way. *"For this is
how God loved the world: He gave **Me**, so that
everyone who believes in **Me** will not perish
but have eternal life.* Does this new viewpoint
change the way you see this verse? If so, how
does it change your view of God's love for us?

_____

_____

_____

_____

_____

_____

When Zeke gave me the picture at the end of the week,
it had an old Argentine Proverb inside (p.53). It read, when
translated, *If you live your life without leaving a mark, for
what are you living it?* As I pondered that, I realized that
as a follower of Christ, despite how complimentary it was
intended to be, that saying as written, was incomplete. Our
lives should read like this, *If we live our lives without leaving
HIS mark, for what are we living it?* (p.54) We are not living
for the moment. We should live as if our lives have an eternal impact. It reminds me of Paul's words in the last part of
II Corinthians 4:18 (NIV),

We fix our gaze on things that cannot be seen.
For the things we see now will soon be gone, but
the things we cannot see will last forever.

Do you really, deep down, believe you can have an eternal impact by leaving *HIS* mark? Specifically, how can you do this?

_____

_____

_____

_____

Who are some people who have left *His* mark on your life?

_____

_____

_____

_____

_____

Name some people upon whom you can have an eternal impact, leaving *HIS* mark.

You <u>can</u> leave HIS mark on the lives of those around you! Consider Paul's words to the Corinthians:

> So, my dear brothers and sisters, be strong and immovable. Always work enthusiastically for the Lord, for you know that *nothing you do for the Lord is ever useless.*
>
> I Corinthians 15:58 (NLT)

CHAPTER 5

RICK'S LEGACY

As we take sports teams to prisons or other countries and compete, people often ask whether or not we let the inmates/locals win? I say, "Nope. We want to win every game we play. We want to be who we say we are, so that our message has credibility. If you come in as a softball team, but can't hit the ball out of the infield, or go to play basketball but you can't make a shot, why would they think anything else we say is true?" (p.56)

Have you ever thought about that? The credibility of your message often depends on *you being who you say you are*. Can people look at every aspect of your life and believe that you are who you say you are? What is an area of your life that doesn't match up with the rest?

_____

_____

_____

_____

_____

Consider the Psalmist's words:

> Oh, that my actions would consistently reflect your decrees!
>
> Psalm 119:5 (NLT)

What role does consistency and/or integrity play in people knowing about your relationship with Christ?

_____

_____

_____

_____

Have you ever let an invitation to church take the place of you sharing the Gospel with someone? Jesus never invited anyone to go to church. He invited them to follow Him. What is the difference?

_____

_____

_____

_____

_____

Wherever we go, we always want to "personalize" the Gospel. What does that mean to you?

_____

_____

_____

_____

_____

_____

_____

In this chapter, we learn about Ramirez, and how despite our team's best efforts and Rick specifically investing in him, he was consistently not ready for a relationship with Jesus (p.58). Are there people in your life like this? How does it make you feel? What can we do about the people in our life like this?

We see what Rick did when he knew it might be the last time we would ever see Ramirez, thus getting one more chance to share with him. *This might be our last shot at Ramirez before he gets out. Start praying now!* (p.60) Have you prayed specifically for people like this before? Seems simple, but so often we leave this part out. Even if we do pray, do we have the same urgency we hear in Rick's voice? If not, why not?

On our fourth visit to Ramirez's prison, he accepted Christ. When asked, "Why now? What was different?" His response was simply, "I don't know, it just clicked this time." Ponder these two verses.

> For no one can come to me unless the Father who sent me draws them to me...
>
> *John 6:44 (NLT)*

> And when I am lifted up from the earth, I will draw all people to myself.
>
> *John 12:32 (NLT)*

In our minds, we as Christians often make sharing our faith too hard, too complicated, or too profound. We scare ourselves out of being obedient. So we ask the following of all of our teams on every trip:

1. Do you think you have the ability to save someone for all eternity?

2. If there's nothing we can do to get it 'right' when we are sharing our faith, don't you think you're being a bit presumptuous or even arrogant to think you can *mess* it up so badly that you can keep someone from coming to Christ, even when He is drawing them?

   So, what are we afraid of? Why do we let fear of not knowing "enough" or not being able to answer a question they might ask keep us from lifting Him up? That is when He draws people to Himself, when we lift Him up. Clearly, we can't get our presentation smooth or polished enough to save someone. There's freedom in that. There's encouragement in that. He simply wants us to be **boldly obedient**. (p.62)

Rick understood that when people step out of their comfort zone and do something bold for Jesus, it gives them a Kingdom Perspective. Your platform or *arena* may not be sports, but we all need a Kingdom perspective. Write down three areas in your life where you need to be **boldly obedient.**

1. _____

_____

_____

2. _____

_____

_____

3. _____

_____

_____

How would your expectations, your understanding or your praying change if you looked at each of those areas above with a Kingdom perspective?

1. _____

_____

2. _____

_____

3. _____

_____

In this chapter, we talked about the legacy that Rick left behind after his death. What does legacy mean to you?

_____

_____

_____

_____

_____

_____

_____

In what parts of your life are you leaving a Godly legacy?

_____

_____

_____

_____

In what parts of your life do you need to change something so that you can leave a Godly legacy? What do you need to change?

_____

_____

_____

One of the reasons Rick was able to leave behind a Godly legacy was because of where his *treasure* was. Read Matthew 6:19-21. Where do your *treasures* lie? Does that need to change? How?

_____

_____

_____

_____

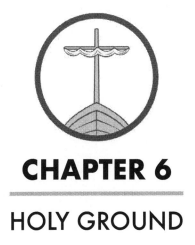

CHAPTER 6

HOLY GROUND

IN EXODUS 3, WE read the story of Moses' encounter with God in the burning bush. While in a hotel room in East Asia, God showed us that the ground around the burning bush was not holy because of God performing a miracle by keeping the bush from burning up despite it being on fire. It was Holy because God Almighty was there. Where God shows up is holy ground, not because of what is going on, but simply because He is there.

Praying for God's presence in the various aspects of our lives will turn it into Holy Ground. How does that change the way you need to pray for:

- Your Spouse:

_____

- Your Kids:

_____

- Your Family:

_____

- Your Friends:

_____

- Your Co-workers:

_____

- Your Teammates:

_____

- Your Neighbor:

_____

Let the enormity of God's words here sink in. Write down what comes to mind as you read them.

> Where were you when I laid the earth's foundation? Tell me, if you understand. Who marked off its dimensions? Surely you know! Who stretched a measuring line across it?

> *Job 38:4-5 (NIV)*

_____

_____

_____

_____

_____

When I read that, I am overwhelmed by how BIG my God is. If you agree, what aspect of your life is too hard for Him to handle or too complicated for Him to show Himself strong?

_____

_____

_____

_____

You may have answered "nothing" to that question, because you feel that's what you are *supposed* to say. But what aspects of your life do you treat as too hard or complicated for God by the way you live? Are you too overwhelmed or consumed to surrender control? What is keeping you from embracing the "Bigness" of God and accepting His control over those circumstances?

_____

_____

_____

_____

For years, we have continued to pray, "God, make this Holy Ground." We have seen God do some incredible things: hearts opened to the Gospel, lives changed for eternity, and even some believers called out to serve in full-time ministry. All because of that simple prayer. If you were bold enough to pray that prayer over your life, what would change? Who would change?

_____

_____

_____

_____

CHAPTER 7

GOD'S SENSE OF HUMOR

IN NUMBERS CHAPTER 22, we read the story of the Moabites summoning Balaam to help them by putting a curse on the invading Israelites. We read that as Balaam began to go to Moab, God put an angel of the Lord in the road to stop him. The donkey upon which he rode could see the angel, but Balaam could not. We then read what has to be one of the funniest moments in Scripture:

> So, the next morning Balaam got up, saddled his donkey, and started off with the Moabite officials. But God was angry that Balaam was going, so he sent the angel of the Lord to stand in the road to block his way.

> As Balaam and two servants were riding along, Balaam's donkey saw the angel of the Lord standing in the road with a drawn sword in his hand. The donkey bolted off the road into a field, but Balaam beat it and turned it back onto the road. Then the angel of the Lord stood at a place where the road narrowed between two vineyard walls. When the donkey saw the angel of the Lord, it tried to squeeze by and crushed Balaam's foot against the wall. So, Balaam beat the donkey again. Then the angel of the Lord moved farther down the road and stood in a place too narrow for the donkey to get by at all.
>
> This time when the donkey saw the angel, it lay down under Balaam. In a fit of rage Balaam beat the animal again with his staff.
>
> Then the Lord gave the donkey the ability to speak. "What have I done to you that deserves your beating me three times?" it asked Balaam.

> Numbers 22: 21-28

It's funny to think about seeing a donkey talking. I mean, who could have ever imagined such a thing taking place. What makes it even funnier is the fact that Balaam talks *back to the donkey* like this was commonplace!

> "You have made me look like a fool!" Balaam shouted. "If I had a sword with me, I would kill you!"

> Numbers 22:29

Of course, as we continue to read we know God allowed Balaam to see what the donkey saw, the angel, with sword drawn. Balaam's first response was to fall face down on the ground. When was the last time you were so overwhelmed by the power and majesty of God that the only thing you could do was to fall on your face? Explain that moment.

For some of us, that doesn't happen enough. For some, it's never happened. Balaam fell face down in worship because he encountered the Almighty God, and in doing so, realized how far short he fell. Complete and total humility in worship was his only response. That's what being *Utterly Amazed* is all about. Encountering the work of God Almighty, and seeing how small we are in comparison. Think of a moment that "just happened" to work out in an incredible way, and the only explanation was God's hand at work? Write it below. Sometimes, we just need to remember God is at work in our lives.

_____

_____

_____

Whether you may immediately remember several times where God intricately worked out the details in your life, or you can't even think of one, there is a key reason we either don't see or don't believe God is at work. We don't think there's a reason for Him to! Apathy is an easy trap for us to fall into. We sometimes forget about our enemy and that we are at war. Consider Paul's words to Timothy:

> Timothy, my son, here are my instructions for you, based on the prophetic words spoken about you earlier. May they help you fight well in the Lord's battles.
>
> I Timothy 1:18 (NLT)

Just like the story in this chapter of how God took car trouble and a seeming disaster to precisely set the stage for Him to come through and remind us of the spiritual war we are in every day, He wants to open our eyes, too.

- What you see as a bad day, He sees as a battle.
- What you see as a difficult time, He sees as a fight.
- What you see as overwhelming odds, He sees as a chance to come through.

What overwhelming odds in your life do you need to see Him come through for you? Write them down. Take a moment to ask Him now to come through for you.

CHAPTER 8

LEE AND JERRY

EACH TIME WE SPEAK about Christ or quote Scripture, we are explaining why we believe what we believe. However, the context can look very different. It can be in a foreign country hostile to the Gospel. It can be speaking to a group here in the US, or simply at a coffee shop talking to a friend, but if we are talking about Jesus or His Word, we are His mouthpiece.

We reviewed in an earlier chapter what Jesus said in John 6:44 (NLT), "For no one can come to me unless the Father who sent me draws them to me."

If we are always His mouthpiece, and we know we can do nothing in ourselves to draw someone to Jesus, we should pray the words of Jesus' to His disciples in Mark 13:11(NLT):

> But when you are arrested and stand trial, don't
> worry in advance about what to say. Just say
> what God tells you at that time, for it is not you
> who will be speaking, but the Holy Spirit.

Father, give me your words. Speak through me. Do you ever de-personalize Scripture? Do you ever look at the people in the Bible as characters, maybe actors playing a role? It's easy for us to forget the people we find in Scripture were real. They had real hurts, real pains, real joys and real laughs. The picture of 12-year old Jesus being left behind in Jerusalem by Mary and Joseph in Luke 2:41-50 is one of those times. We know Jesus is the Son of God, so of course He would be ok by Himself for a few days! Put yourself in Mary or Joseph's shoes. Your kid has been missing for 5 days, in the largest city you've ever seen, during the time of Passover celebration when the city is slammed with visitors. In reality, there was little to no way they were ever going to find Jesus, and you had to believe that Mary and Joseph's hope was fading as the days passed.

Take a minute and rewrite this encounter in your own words as if it had happened to you. What if this was your child or your responsibility? What would you be feeling? What would you be thinking? What would you have done when you found 12-year old Jesus after five LONG days?

In this light-hearted exercise, don't miss Jesus' response to his mother in Luke 2:49 (NKJV):

> And He said to them, "Why did you seek Me? Did you not know that I must be about My Father's business?"

> As a Christ-Follower, we should always be about our Father's business, wherever that takes us, and should also never feel anxious about sharing the Truth. "Just say what God tells you at that time, for it is not you who will be speaking, but the Holy Spirit." Mark 13:1 (NLT) (p. 83).

How does it make you feel, to know that God can speak His words through you, even an eternal invitation, to someone? How does that change the way you see you sharing your faith?

_____

_____

_____

_____

_____

_____

When Lee met Jerry that day in the gym on his campus, God presented Jerry with an eternal invitation through Lee's diminishing language skills. I don't think she expected God to give that invitation in Jerry's heart language, but Lee's prayer was that God would speak through her. (p.83-85)

Combine these two thoughts: You must always be about your Father's business, AND God wants to make His appeal to the world through you. Let that sink in. Now write down 3 ways that this might happen in your life if you were bold enough to pray for those two thoughts.

1. _____

_____

_____

2. _____

_____

_____

3. _____

_____

_____

CHAPTER 9

MY WAYS ARE HIGHER

"My thoughts are nothing like your thoughts,"
says the Lord. "And my ways are far beyond
anything you could imagine. For just as the
heavens are higher than the earth, so my ways
are higher than your ways and my thoughts are
higher than your thoughts."

Isaiah 55:8-9 (NLT)

You've probably heard someone use this passage before, or maybe you have even used it yourself. Usually, it's trying to explain something they don't understand about God or what's happening in their life or the life of someone they know. For example, my daughter was born with cancer. She started chemo shortly after she was born. She had several major subsequent surgeries, and during the entire time, people were quoting this verse to my wife and me. Though I knew it to be true, if I'm being honest, it didn't necessarily make me feel much better at the moment. I knew it in my head and my heart, but my heart still hurt, and there was still a mountain of fear and anxiety weighing down on us. (Just so you know, she is a thriving young adult now!)

There isn't anything inherently wrong with fear or hurt or uncertainty. We know that Jesus wept for His friend Lazarus when he died, when he saw how much Mary and Martha were hurting. We know he sweat drops of blood in the Garden the night before his crucifixion, which can only happen in times of extreme anguish and anxiety. To hurt or worry in the moment of trial is to be human. However, your worldview, your overall perspective of this world and your life must reflect this truth of Isaiah 55:8-9, if your hope truly is in Him. We don't always have the answers, but we know who does, and we believe He knows better than us anyway!

What is going on in your life right now that you just have to trust the words of God though the prophet Isaiah? Are you trusting Him with it?

Trusting God knows better than we do doesn't just apply to hardship. It can apply to every aspect of your life. When you lose your job, His ways are higher. When your friend turns his back on you, His ways are higher. When your child doesn't want to follow the path you think they should follow, His ways are higher. When your marriage is on the rocks, His ways are higher. When a loved one's health is fading, His ways are higher.

Is there really a plan bigger than simply what you can see? Write down an area of your life where you are really struggling with fear, doubt and anxiety. Then ask God to help you release that to Him. Trust Him with the answer.

_____

_____

_____

_____

On our trip to South Asia, things didn't work out like we had hoped. We had prayed for many opportunities to share our faith. We had just one. We were worried about the government and how hostile they were to Christians. The Governor was the only one with whom we had the chance to share. Our team was obedient in the one chance they had to share and it led to the governor asking us to send coaches to live and work there full-time! We thought the doors were shut, but God knew better. He used the situation we wouldn't have chosen to do more than we could imagine!

Now all glory to God, who is able, through his mighty power at work within us, to accomplish infinitely more than we might ask or think.

Ephesians 3:20 (NLT)

Where in your life do you need God to do infinitely more than you could ask or think? List as many areas as you can. Are you trusting Him with each one? How can you trust Him more?

_____

_____

_____

_____

_____

_____

_____

_____

_____

CHAPTER 10

OLE HENRY

WHEREVER WE GO, WE always want to personalize Jesus. I have been called a minister or a missionary, so one would think talking about Jesus is my job. "Of course, you're supposed to say those things." Because of that, when we travel to prisons or places overseas that are not restricted to the Gospel, we always want to have one of our group tell their story of what Christ has done in their lives. We want to make sure people understand that Jesus is not a part of a particular ministry, denomination, or church. He is above all of those things, and He is not limited by them.

Jesus' passion and purpose were to go to those that needed Him wherever that may be, not to build a church. Consider His words in Matthew 9:10-13 (NLT):

> Later, Matthew invited Jesus and his disciples to his home as dinner guests, along with many tax collectors and other disreputable sinners. But when the Pharisees saw this, they asked his disciples, "Why does your teacher eat with such *scum*?" When Jesus heard this, he said, "Healthy people don't need a doctor—sick people do." Then he added, "Now go and learn the meaning of this Scripture: I want you to show mercy, not offer sacrifices. For I have come to call not those who think they are righteous, but those who *know* they are sinners."

Jesus went to the hurting and the lost. Jesus went to the broken, no matter the social ramifications. The Pharisees called Matthew and his friends, *scum*. Jesus didn't care what the Pharisees said, because these people were for whom He had come. Jesus came for the sick, because He had the cure. He *was* the cure!

If Jesus was the cure, how could He not go to the "sick?" If you belong to Jesus, YOU now have the cure! Think about you having a cure for the world, for an other wise incurable disease.

How does this change the way you see and/or approach the lost?

_____

_____

_____

_____

_____

_____

What is your role in sharing that cure with the world?

_____

_____

_____

_____

_____

_____

What do His words to the Pharisees during this encounter mean? "I want you to show mercy, not offer sacrifices."

_____

_____

_____

_____

_____

What traditions or rituals have you let get in the way of your walk with Jesus? How has The Church done the same?

_____

_____

_____

_____

_____

_____

Allow me to modernize it a little. Jesus is saying,
"I want your heart. I don't want your routine.
I want you to live like me daily, not just go
through the motions on Sunday. Find those that
are 'sick' and show me to them by the way you
live your lives." (p. 98)

That day in a Florida state prison when Henry met Jesus for the first time, God called Henry to His side. He didn't take Henry out of the prison. Henry's sentence wasn't reduced as far as I know. However, he was set free even though he was still behind those walls (p.101). Do you believe Jesus will save someone who's done something as awful as Henry? Read 2 Corinthians 5:17 (NLT):

This means that anyone who belongs to Christ
has become a new person. The old life is gone;
a new life has begun!

Write it below and then answer this question. What is the significance of "anyone" or "any man?"

_____

_____

_____

_____

_____

Read James 2:10 (NLT):

> For the person who keeps all of the laws except one is as guilty as a person who has broken all of God's laws.

Let that sink in. Write it down below and then answer this question. How are we any different in God's eyes from Double Homicide Henry?

_____

_____

_____

_____

_____

_____

_____

_____

_____

CHAPTER 11

SMART MICHAEL

PREVIOUSLY, I TALKED ABOUT how important it is to personalize the mission, to put a face and a name on each of the countless billions who still don't know Jesus, many whom have never heard before. Usually, I am the one coming back telling others about those we've encountered, shared with and prayed for. However, Smart Michael's story started differently. I heard about him from a volunteer leading a trip of which I was not a part. After spending some time with our volunteer trip leader, I felt like I knew Smart Michael. I had someone specific to pray for. I had seen his face in pictures. I knew his story.

How does it change your prayer when you know the person you're praying for?

_____

_____

_____

_____

_____

If putting a face with a name changes the way you pray, what can you do about praying specifically for the lost?

_____

_____

_____

_____

After spending some time with Smart Michael, I realized just how fitting his nickname was. He had struggled getting to a point of trusting Jesus, because he was trying to figure Jesus out. You can't *figure* Jesus out. In fact, Jesus says in Matthew 18:3 (NLT):

> I tell you the truth, unless you turn from your sins and become like little children, you will never get into the Kingdom of Heaven.

That's where faith comes in. There are aspects of God's character, parts of His will for our lives we just can't understand. Children don't need all the answers. We just have to trust. Where in your life is it hard to trust Jesus right now?

_____

_____

_____

_____

We all have things in Scripture we don't understand. There are things about our world today we would love to ask of God. What are some of your questions?

_____

_____

_____

_____

There were dozens of people praying for Smart Michael between our first trip and second trip to his city. We prayed for him to come to a point of surrender, that he would realize he could never fully understand God, but would trust Him anyway. When he finally came into our hotel room one morning late in the second trip and said he was "ready for Jesus" (p.117), it seemed similar to the moment when the Lord freed Peter from prison. He immediately went to see the Believers who had been praying for him in Acts 12:6-16. When the little girl, Rhoda, came in and told everyone Peter was at the door, they called her crazy! God had answered their specific prayer and they called the messenger "crazy!"

What have you been praying for, only out of a sense of duty, because you were taught that's what Christians are supposed to do? Do you believe God will or even can answer that prayer?

_____

_____

_____

_____

Confess your doubts to God below and then pray the same prayer the father of the demon-possessed boy prayed in Mark 9:24 (NLT).

> "What do you mean, 'If I can'?" Jesus asked. "Anything is possible if a person believes." The father instantly cried out, "I do believe, but help me overcome my unbelief!"

_____

_____

_____

CHAPTER 12

I'M NOT READY

THE AVERAGE SIZE OF one of our international teams is about seven. The average size of a prison trip is about twelve. Through the years, for every "yes" we might get, we have also averaged about seven that decline. That means, on average, we have to ask about 56 people in order to fill an international team (p.121)! Why do so many say no? Money? Work? Conflicts with other obligations? Yes, yes and yes. However, there is another reason even more common, and it has nothing to do with cost or time. It is simply the feeling that "I'm not ready."

Everyone reading through this study can understand doubt, and the belief that you're not qualified to be a vessel through which Jesus reaches the nations.

> We must get past, "I'm not ready." That doesn't just mean committing to go on a trip, but also moving toward the boundaries of what you think you can do in the name of Jesus, then surpassing those boundaries! (p. 123)

Ask yourself this question. What is it that I KNOW God is moving/asking me to do but I haven't yet because I'm not qualified?

That sense of being unqualified or disqualified comes from a warped, human sense of identity. When you say "I'm not ready to _____," you are also saying that God is not a factor in any part of this decision. If "I'm not ready" is your reason for disobeying God, you are saying He has nothing to do with it. He cannot use you right now. You are too focused on *who* you are (or aren't) and not *Whose* you are.

Each time He said, "My grace is all you need. My power works best in weakness." So now I am glad to boast about my weaknesses, so that the power of Christ can work through me.

II Corinthians 12:9 (NLT)

Paul realized his effectiveness as a messenger of the Gospel did not depend on who he was or what he had to offer. His effectiveness was found in Christ working through him. How effective are you currently as a messenger of the Gospel?

_____

_____

_____

_____

_____

If we feel unqualified or "not ready," it is because we've either not grasped the fact that God *wants* to use us, or we feel guilt/shame because of our past. I think we all can agree that if God *wants* to use us, He can. He said He would make the rocks cry out, so I think He can use me. If He can hold the seas in place, He can use me. If He spoke the universe into existence, I believe He can use me.

He used Jeremy. Go back and read the last two paragraphs in "Jeremy's" section on pages 125-126. Think about all those watching him get baptized and then immediately commissioned for his first mission trip. They were all thinking he wasn't ready.

> That line of thinking is what has kept millions of Christians stuck to their pews across the generations. The truth is, we will never be ready. There's nothing we can do to save anyone. Only God Almighty through the resurrection of His son can do that. We just have to be faithful in pointing people to Him, just like Jeremy was, regardless of whether we are ready. (p. 126)

Getting past our guilt and shame is a bit trickier, because it's a two-step process. We see it in the story of Lazarus. We know that if we choose to surrender our lives to Jesus, spiritually speaking, we are raised to a new life. Read John 11:32-44. In v. 43 (NLT), Jesus tells Lazarus to come out of the grave. "Then Jesus shouted, "Lazarus, come out!"

That is the same picture when God called us out of the grave. We walk out of the tomb into a new life. That is the first step. But then look at v. 44 (NLT).

> And the dead man came out, his hands and feet bound in graveclothes, his face wrapped in a head cloth. Jesus told them, "Unwrap him and let him go!"

Lazarus had to take the graveclothes off, and he needed help to do it. Too many of us are still walking around with graveclothes on, the shame and guilt of our past. We haven't sought help from fellow believers or from God to shed them. We walk around, alive, but still bound by our graveclothes. That shame and guilt disqualifies us in our minds. But note who gave the order to remove the grave clothes…JESUS!! He freed us from death, but He didn't do it so we could walk around still bound.

What "graveclothes" do you need to remove?

What is keeping you from removing them? Do you need help? Name someone(s) you can ask for help. Then ask them!

Once you've grasped that God Almighty wants to use *you*, and you've removed the graveclothes that may have been holding you back, take a note from Marcy's story on p.130. *Marcy was not ready for the game…but she was ready for the mission. She was walking out on that softball field confident, not in her ability, but in the one who gave her her ability!*

But let us who live in the light be clear headed,
protected by the armor of faith and love,
and wearing as our helmet the *confidence of
our salvation.*

I Thessalonians 5:8 (NLT)

Marcy wasn't polished. She certainly wasn't
prepared. Marcy wasn't ready, but she knew
her God was! (p. 131)

In what part of your life could you use more confidence. Write it down. Now ask God to give you that needed confidence.

_____

_____

_____

_____

_____

_____

_____

_____

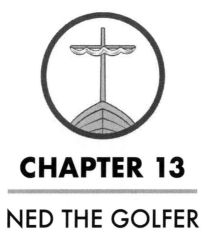

CHAPTER 13

NED THE GOLFER

AS WE HAVE TRAVELED, we have met and spent time with people from every major world religion, and even some not so "major." The common theme among each of them is there is no room for investigation or questions. Remember the Basketball Executive in SE Asia who was a devout Buddhist?

> When we pressed him on his answers about his religion, he responded simply, "Buddha says 'don't ask questions that have no answers'." (p. 134)

Usually when people don't want you to ask questions, or they resist investigation, they are trying to hide something. There's not a hint of that with God. In fact, it's the exact opposite.

> "You will seek me and find me when you seek me with all your heart. I will be found by you," declares the Lord, "and will bring you back from captivity."
>
> *Jeremiah 29:13-14a (NIV)*

> *Keep on asking,* and you will receive what you ask for. *Keep on seeking,* and you will find. *Keep on knocking,* and the door will be opened to you. For everyone who *asks,* receives. Everyone who *seeks,* finds. And to everyone who *knocks,* the door will be opened.
>
> *Matthew 7:7-8 (NLT)*

Jesus is giving us the freedom to question, the freedom to pursue truth. He's not afraid of you chasing after the truth. He is the Truth! What are the things you find in Scripture, or you have found in your daily life that you struggle with and want to ask God about?

I love the NLT's version of Matthew 7:7-8. It says to *keep on* asking, seeking and knocking. It's a picture of continuous action, but it is also a picture of God's patience with us. Read Peter's words in II Peter 3:9 (NLT):

> The Lord isn't really being slow about His promise, as some people think. No, He is being patient for your sake. He does not want anyone to be destroyed, but wants everyone to repent.

In regards to your questions, wonderings or searching, how does this passage change your thinking?

_____

_____

_____

_____

_____

_____

_____

_____

_____

In this story of Ned's miraculous journey to get to East Asia with us (p.137), his lack of basketball qualifications was not something to be overlooked. Yet God, in His infinite wisdom, decided to use the unlikeliest of the group in an unlikely place, in a miraculous way.

> But to those called by God to salvation, both Jews and Gentiles, Christ is the power of God and the wisdom of God. This foolish plan of God is wiser than the wisest of human plans, and God's weakness is stronger than the greatest of human strength.
>
> I Corinthians 1:24-25 (NLT)

That means, if you are a follower of Jesus, it doesn't matter how unqualified you think you are, the power and wisdom of God are yours! Think about that for a moment. *Power and wisdom* are both things we often feel are lacking in our everyday lives, but they are actually ours to use. Think about a place where you are struggling, or a place where you could be used. How does having access to God's power and wisdom change your thinking?

_____

_____

_____

_____

When it came to basketball skill or knowledge, Ned was the weakest in our group. One would probably not have chosen him for this task, but even the foolish plans of God are wiser than any of ours, and his weakness is stronger than any strength we may have.

> The Lord says, "I will guide you along the best pathway for your life. I will advise you and watch over you."
>
> *Psalm 32:8 (NLT)*

How does God using Ned instead of others more qualified, and the truth in David's words above, shed light on God's plan for your life? How does it change your willingness to seek hard after that plan?

_____

_____

_____

_____

_____

_____

_____

CHAPTER 14

AARON—FROM OPPONENT TO TEAMMATE

IN THE COUNTRY WHERE we met Aaron, there was a significant presence of three major world religions. It was not unusual to see a Buddhist Temple, a Hindu Temple, and a Mosque all on the same block (p.142). This was a reminder of my encounter with the Chief in Ghana back in Chapter 1, and the manifestation of Romans 1:19-20 (NLT).

> They know the truth about God because He has made it obvious to them. For ever since the world was created, people have seen the

earth and sky. Through everything God made, they can clearly see his invisible qualities—His eternal power and divine nature. So, they have no excuse for not knowing God.

How does this picture of Temples and Mosques on the same street illustrate Paul's word in Romans 1?

_____

_____

_____

_____

On p.143, we see a picture of my wife on the sideline wanting to participate, but not being able to. She could not use her obvious athletic gifts to make a difference. This is something we can encounter often in our lives. It could be a physical limitation such as in her story, or it could be circumstances beyond our control. When you want to, but are unable to participate in making a difference with the gifts with which God has equipped you, how does it make you feel?

_____

_____

_____

_____

When we feel inadequate for whatever reason, it is almost always the voice of the enemy. That self-doubt is a tool used to keep us on the sideline, but just like in my wife's case, maybe the "sideline" is exactly where He wants you! Have you ever been "sidelined" and God still used you? How?

_____

_____

_____

_____

_____

Have you ever let being "sidelined" frustrate you and keep you from being used? How?

_____

_____

_____

_____

_____

When Aaron asked my wife if she was a Christian on p.145, she clarified by saying that she was a "Follower of Jesus." The term Christian is misused and misunderstood around the world. She then went on to explain what being a "Follower of Jesus" meant to her. What does being a "Follower of Jesus" mean to you?

When given the chance to finally explain to Aaron what being a "follower" meant, this is what she said.

> "... growing up in Christian church with Christian parents, making a decision to ask Jesus into her life at the age of eight, but then not truly giving up control of her life until she was 29-years-old. She shared her story of being around and

loving the things and people of God for two decades, but that she never really gave up control of her life until the night before her one-year-old daughter was facing a life-threatening surgery. It was that night she realized she had been trying to do everything in her own power. She had maintained control of her life, despite asking Jesus to save her from her sin years ago. She knew she couldn't walk through what she was about to face without Jesus being the Lord of her life, and giving Him control of her heart, her mind, and her actions. She then shared with Aaron that, "That night, down at the end of the hospital hallway, I dropped to my knees, all alone, and through my tears, I told Jesus he could have everything: my heart, my life, my future, my daughter. That's what following Jesus means to me." (pp. 145-146)

In the Church, it is common to interchange the words "Lord" and "Savior," but they mean two very different things. *Savior* literally means "ones who saves." We like that. We want to be "saved" from our sin and from hell. *Lord* is very different. Lord means "a person who has authority, control, or power over others." That means if Jesus truly is your *Lord*, you have no authority over your own life. You give up control to Him, which is a little harder to embrace. That was my wife's story, and when she shared it with Aaron, note his response, "I've never heard anyone talk like this before, no matter if they were Christian, Muslim or Buddhist" (p. 146).

Seeing life change is what inspires more life change. The best tool for doing our part in seeing those around us come to know Jesus is to know our story of life change, and be able to share it effectively. Consider your own story around these three thoughts:

1. What was your life like before you surrendered to Christ?
2. What was that moment of surrender like?
3. What has your life been like since you surrendered to Him?

Take a few minutes and write down these three parts of your story of life change (a.k.a. your testimony).

1. _____

   _____

2. _____

   _____

3. _____

   _____

After you write it down, share it with someone. Practice it. Be ready to share it.

If someone asks about your hope as a believer, always be ready to explain it.

I Peter 3:15 (NLT)

CHAPTER 15

RICH THE POLICEMAN

MANY IMAGES COME TO mind when we think about the Last Supper, the last meal that Jesus had with His disciples before he was arrested and then crucified. I know for me, one of those images is NOT Jesus praying for *me* 2,000 years before I was born!

> I am praying not only for these disciples but also for all who will ever believe in me through their message.
>
> *John 17:20 (NLT)*

Don't rush past this. Take a few minutes and contemplate the significance of this prayer. On the night Jesus was arrested, the night before He was going to be scourged, shamed, mocked and crucified, *you* were on His mind. He prayed for *you*! He also prayed for the Church.

> I pray that they will all be one, just as you and I are one—as you are in me, Father, and I am in you... I am in them and you are in me. May they experience such perfect unity that the world will know that you sent me and that you love them as much as you love me.
>
> *John 17:21, 23 (NLT)*

Jesus prayed we would have the unity that He and the Father enjoyed! If you look at the Church today, where do you see that unity? Where is it missing?

When you think you don't have what it takes to be His witness in a particular moment, or to make it through a rough season in your life, remember Jesus has already prayed for you! How does that change your thinking?

In Rich's story in this chapter (p.154), he struggled initially because what he thought he knew about Christians didn't line up with the followers of Christ with whom he was now spending time. He saw Jesus in our team; not only in what we said, but in how we treated each other. When an unbelieving world looks at the Church, they make decisions about us based on what we do, and how we care for each other. Do you think the world sees that when they look at The Church? What else *should* they see when they look at us?

Two years after Rich chose to follow Jesus, we met back up with him, and ultimately, we had the chance to baptize him. What always amazes me on our trips through the years is how time and geography have very little impact, when Christ is what connects us. Two years after Rich made the most important decision of his life, we met back up as if no time had passed.

When you look at your relationships with other believers, do you enjoy that kind of Christ connection? Are you friends because of your relationships with Christ and you work together in making His name known, or are you friends who also just happen to also be followers of Jesus?

How can we make these relationships stronger?

We put boundaries on God when we make excuses as to why we can't share our faith, or we question how God could use us in drawing someone to His side for all eternity. We put a limit on His sovereignty, His wisdom, and His ability to use whomever or whatever He wants in order to accomplish His purpose. How does this change your mind about *if* and *how* God can use you?

CHAPTER 16

SECRET CHURCH

What is it like to worship in a place where you can be arrested, beaten, ostracized or even killed for your faith?

For most of us here in the US, that is such a foreign concept, it's hard to grasp and we certainly can't truly understand. We have known nothing but religious freedom our entire lives. That is not anything to be sorry for. But sometimes, those freedoms blind us from the privilege it really is to gather freely to worship. (pp. 157-158)

When comparing your worship gatherings to the ones talked about in this chapter, what is different? What is the same?

_____

_____

_____

_____

> Let us hold tightly without wavering to the hope we affirm, for God can be trusted to keep his promise. Let us think of ways to motivate one another to acts of love and good works. And let us not neglect our meeting together, as some people do, but encourage one another, especially now that the day of his return is drawing near.
>
> *Hebrews 10:23-25 (NLT)*

These verses are a picture of what The Church should look like. List three attributes of the church found in this passage.

1. _____

2. _____

3. _____

All other world religions have issues with Christianity. They are tolerant of other religions, just not Christianity. Why? It's because of Jesus' words in John 14:6 (NLT) "I am the way, the truth, and the life. *No one* can come to the Father except through me." There is no in-between with Jesus. There can't be "your truth" and "my truth." There is only The Truth, and The Truth is Jesus. How has our society's insistence on everyone having their own "truth" obscured people's view of The Truth?

_____

_____

_____

_____

_____

What are some of the dangers of everyone having their own "truth?"

_____

_____

_____

_____

_____

What I admired most about these secret churches was a hunger, a humility, and a reverence for God's word that we seldom model here in the US. Their devotion and commitment to Christ, regardless of the cost, made me challenge everything. How does it challenge you? Using a scale of 1-5, with 5 being the highest, rate yourself on the following items.

- _____ A hunger for God's word
- _____ Humility among the Body of Christ
- _____ Reverence for God's word
- _____ Commitment to meet with other believers
- _____ Commitment to share my faith

The common theme among these secret churches is that they keep the main thing the main thing. This is what Paul meant in I Corinthians 2:2 (NLT):

> For I decided that while I was with you I would forget everything except Jesus Christ, the one who was crucified.

"Forget everything else except Jesus Christ." Imagine what our churches would be like if we all chased that as our goal? What would *your* life look like if you did? What would *your* church look like?

Personally, one of my favorite parts of this journey we have been on for almost 20 years are the places where I have been able to speak/teach/preach— places where the Gospel had to be translated, where people don't speak like me, worship like me, or look like me. (p. 164)

How does this compare to our church demographics in the US?

_____

_____

_____

_____

Why do you think our church services look so homogeneous throughout denominations? Should they change? How can you help that change?

_____

_____

_____

_____

_____

_____

> As Scripture says, "Anyone who believes in
> him will never be put to shame." For there is no
> difference between Jew and Gentile—the same
> Lord is Lord of all and richly blesses all who call
> on him, for, "Everyone who calls on the name of
> the Lord will be saved."

Romans 10:11-13 (NIV)

Is God calling you to be a part of the Great Commission? I'm going to help you here. You don't even need to wrestle with an answer to that question! Your answer, if you call yourself a follower of Christ MUST be "yes!" We as the Church, the Bride of Christ, have let that task fall on the "professionals" for far too long. This whole study has been a journey to help you find where God is calling you. Not *if* but *WHERE!* Has the picture of God's plan for your life become any more clearer to you? Write down what you are seeing.

_____

_____

_____

_____

_____

_____

CHAPTER 17

WHAT'S THIS WORD?

HALF OF THE WORLD'S population lives in a place where ninety-eight percent of the people around them do not follow Jesus, mostly due to factors such as government, geography, or culture. Four billion people world-wide have little to no access to the Gospel. These numbers can be overwhelming, so unfortunately, they stay just that, numbers. We want you to know Xing Xing. We want you to see Nyan Lin. We want you to know Mohan or Jhanani. We want you to see more than just statistics, because they are certainly more than just numbers!

Go back and read the paragraph starting at the bottom of p.167, where I talk about seeing kids in-between classes. I never noticed specific kids in the sea of humanity that passed by my classroom until I met them personally. That is how we approach the task of the Great Commission. It must become personal for us. We need to personalize it for others. How do *we* do that? List some ways *you* can personalize the Great Commission for yourself.

Regardless of what form fulfilling the Great Commission ends up taking for you, all of us need a greater sense of urgency. In this chapter's story (p.169), our team soon realized that playing this country's national team was not going to be as glamorous and challenging as once believed. Fortunately, our team knew their time for building relationships and sharing Jesus was limited, so there became a greater sense of urgency off the court.

What level of urgency do you feel for the eternal well-being of those around you daily? Does it need to change? Why? How?

_____

_____

_____

_____

_____

_____

_____

_____

_____

> Our girls got to know their girls better. As is the
> case in most of these conversational scenarios,
> when you begin to talk about family and
> friends and what's important to you and your
> backstory, we encourage our folks to begin to
> share about their faith (p. 169).

I challenge you to do the same. If your relationship with Jesus is the most important thing to you, then it should organically come up in conversation (and not just on a mission trip).

Write down the names of two people in your circle of friends who don't know Jesus. If intentional, how can you steer a normal conversation towards Jesus? Consider how your conversation strategy may change for different situations or people. For example, you would probably have a different conversation with someone at work than with someone at the gym. What conversation ideas do you have for the names you wrote below? Be specific.

_____

_____

_____

_____

_____

_____

Terri said, "Well, first of all, I already love
MM, and I've only known her for three days! I
feel like the Lord has already given me a deep
burden for her." I told her, "That's not unusual.
When we are focused on the task, and we begin
to see people the way Jesus sees them, we can't
help but be burdened, especially in a place like
this." (p.170)

Terri began to see MM the way Jesus sees MM, someone He died for, someone He ransomed with His life.
Asking God to open your eyes to see people as He does
makes all the difference.

What are you doing to personalize the *Nations* so you
see the individual needs? What else can you do?

_____

_____

_____

_____

_____

_____

_____

_____

What are you doing to personalize those close by, so you can see them the way God does? What else can you do?

CHAPTER 18

WHY DO YOU KEEP GOING?

MOST CHRISTIANS, AND SUBSEQUENTLY, most churches measure ministry success numerically. If the numbers aren't impressive, the project wasn't a success. The larger a church, the more successful it is. It is difficult to escape this way of thinking. In the context of a mission trip then, what happens if no one accepts Christ and becomes a believer? What if you didn't have the chance to verbally share the Gospel even once? Think about this as you read the story of the shepherd and his 100 sheep in Matthew 18:12-14 (NLT):

If a man has a hundred sheep and one of them wanders away, what will he do? Won't he leave the ninety-nine others on the hills and go out to search for the one that is lost? And if he finds it, I tell you the truth, he will rejoice over it more than over the ninety-nine that didn't wander away! In the same way, it is not my heavenly Father's will that even one of these little ones should perish.

Why do you think Jesus makes the point here that the shepherd left the ninety-nine to go look for the one?

_____

_____

_____

_____

Knowing that Jesus is the shepherd in the story, what does this mean to you and the mission?

_____

_____

_____

_____

Consider the story of Jorge from Nicaragua on pp.174-175. Halfway through our trip, he was the only person to have accepted Christ. Jason expressed his frustration mid-trip about Jorge being the only new believer. The question was raised, "If this trip was just for Jorge, would it have been worth it? "As followers of Jesus, or even just obedient church-goers, we know we are supposed to say yes. However, are we always being honest about how we feel as we answer? Thirteen guys went on this trip. The per-person cost was approximately $1800. That means, collectively over $23,000 was spent so that Jorge could have the chance to choose Jesus. Was it truly worth it? Should we have devoted our resources elsewhere, somewhere that we could possibly see more results? Describe your thoughts if you were on that trip?

In W's story, beginning on p.175, we see something that can't be disregarded. We had served with him on three different trips. During those trips, six of our guys had the opportunity to share the Gospel with him. Several of them had stayed in contact with W even after we returned home. The local brothers had also invested countless hours in W, sharing the Gospel story, but also just diving into Scripture at their Bible studies. Yet W was *still* not ready to choose Jesus! List below some reasons you've heard for people not deciding to follow Jesus.

_____

_____

_____

_____

_____

_____

_____

Some reasons people give may seem illegitimate in your opinion, and you might be right! But in their eyes, those reasons are still legitimate and are significant obstacles to them, regardless of our opinions. Instead of becoming frustrated with their "excuses," we need to look for ways to help them see past those obstacles.

In W's case, if he chose to follow Jesus, he would potentially be forced to give up his family *and* his future! Put yourself in his position. If you were W, what would you need to hear that would make you change your mind?

_____

_____

_____

_____

Consider Paul's response to the church in Corinth when he heard them saying things like "I'm a follower of Paul. Well, I'm a follower of Apollos."

> After all, who is Apollos? Who is Paul? We are only God's servants through whom you believed the Good News. *Each of us did the work the Lord gave us.* I planted the seed in your hearts, and Apollos watered it, but *it was God who made it grow.* It's not important who does the planting, or who does the watering. What's important is that God makes the seed grow. The one who plants and the one who waters *work together with the same purpose.* And both will be rewarded for their own hard work. For we are both God's workers. And you are God's field. You are God's building.
>
> *I Corinthians 3:5-9 (NLT)*

Consider these three phrases from the passage. Below them, describe the significance of each statement.

1. "Each of us did the work the Lord gave us."
2. "It was God who made it grow."
3. "Work together with the same purpose."

1. _____

_____

2. _____

_____

3. _____

_____

If *The Church* believed these three statements, we would change the world! In the meantime, how can you help change the minds of the people in your sphere of influence so they truly believe these three statements? Don't just say, "I can't." You can!

_____

_____

_____

_____

CONCLUSION

PRODUCTIVE DISCOMFORT

WHEN IT COMES TO working out, you have to first tear down the muscle to achieve growth. Growth comes from discomfort. It's true physiologically, but it's also true spiritually. Describe how you have seen this happen in your own life.

How has the concept of "getting out of your comfort zone" been glamorized in The Church? Do we celebrate those who get out of their comfort zone, or do we celebrate what happens *after* they step out? Which is more significant?

_____

_____

_____

_____

Inertia is defined as "inactivity, sluggishness and inertness, especially with regard to effort, motion, action, and the like." How does inertia affect our efforts to grow the Kingdom? How can staying in our comfort zone affect these efforts?

_____

_____

_____

_____

_____

As we conclude our study, I hope you are seeing the growth that can happen as a result of stepping out of your comfort zone. What you do while outside of your comfort zone truly makes the difference. We don't take people out of their comfort zones just so we can say we made them uncomfortable. We want to draw people out of their existing comfort zones (or boats) so *we can plug them into a new place where they are comfortable.* The next step in your growth, towards becoming the man or woman whom God has created you to be, is learning how to use the gifts and passions He has given you for His glory.

Name some things you love to do for fun, for work, as a hobby and for recreation.

_____

_____

_____

_____

_____

_____

_____

_____

_____

Now name some ways, places, people, or contexts where you could use the above list to help grow the Kingdom. Take your time and really think deeply about ways to match your passions with God's desire for all to come to know Him.

_____

_____

_____

_____

_____

_____

Think back to the story of Peter walking on the water in Matthew 14. He wanted to be with Jesus so much, he was willing to risk doing something everyone else thought was crazy and weren't willing to do themselves. Peter didn't care. He had his eyes focused on Jesus and what Jesus could do through him, not what everyone else was saying.

Maybe it's time for you to risk doing something for the cause of Christ, that seems crazy to everyone else. Maybe it's time for you to use the gifts and the skills that God has given you to *impact* the world for Him? There are billions of people waiting for you.

By now, you probably already know what that "crazy something" is. Look back at what you wrote down on page

xii. Has it become any more real or possible while doing this study? Have you done it or taken steps towards it? If not, what is stopping you?

Reread Matthew 9:36-38 (NLT) below.

> When He saw the crowds, he had compassion on them because they were confused and helpless, like sheep without a shepherd. He said to his disciples, *"The harvest is great, but the workers are few.* So, pray to the Lord who is in charge of the harvest; ask Him to send more workers into His fields."

"The harvest is great, but the workers are few." Let me remind you of some stats from thetravelingteam.org I shared with you at the beginning of this journey:

- Over 3 Billion people on the planet have *never* heard the name of Jesus…not even once!
- Over 4 Billion have *no access to the Gospel!*
- Of the 400,000 cross-cultural missionaries working worldwide, *only **three percent** go to the unreached!*
- Only $1 of every $100,000 that Christians earn is going to reach the unreached, 42.5 percent of the world!

Are these just numbers to you, or do they mean more to you now? As followers of Jesus Christ, tasked by Him to use what we have to reach the nations, they must become more than just numbers.

How has God changed your heart and understanding of the global need since you started this study?

What is going to be your response to this global need? Are you going to go? Are you going to give? Wherever you feel like God is leading you, there are billions of people counting on you to follow through. You may not be able to see the end, but I hope by now you can at least see the beginning of your "stepping out of the boat" story. You don't have to go with us, but step out the boat and *go* somewhere! What is your first "step out of the boat?"

WHO IS
JOHN ANDREWS?

AS I MENTIONED AT the beginning of the book, we had to change the names and locations in the book for their protection and ours. That includes me. John Andrews is not my birth name. I chose the name based on the story we find in John 1:35-42.

John the Baptist was prophesied about in the Old Testament. He was Jesus' cousin. We read about him in Luke 1 before he was even born. We know that he had developed quite a following as the forerunner to Jesus, the one who was supposed to prepare the way for the Lord's coming. Jesus came to *him* to be baptized. If anyone had the right to pat themselves on the back a little, it was John the Baptist but that's not who he was.

Look at John 1:35-37 (NLT):

> The following day John was again standing with two of his disciples. As Jesus walked by, John looked at him and declared, "Look! There is the Lamb of God!" When John's two disciples heard this, they followed Jesus.

John told *his* disciples to turn and look at Jesus, "take your eyes off of me," knowing that if they spent time with Jesus, they would probably never return to him. That's who we should be as followers of Jesus; men and women who will point people to Jesus no matter what the cost will be to us.

Now look at who one of those two disciples was and what he did first:

> **Andrew,** Simon Peter's brother, was one of these men who heard what John said and then followed Jesus. Andrew went to find his brother, Simon, and told him, "We have found the Messiah" (which means "Christ"). *Then Andrew brought Simon to meet Jesus.*
>
> *John 1:40-42a (NLT)*

The second step in following Jesus is what Andrew did next. After spending time with Jesus, he left to go find those closest to him and bring them to Jesus.

This is where John Andrews comes from. We should want to point people to Jesus AND bring others along in their journey with Him. During the adventure of writing this book and study guide, God made one thing very clear to me. "There is nothing special about the author, John Andrews. He is just someone who was willing to step out of his boat, and I wrote *My story* in and through him."

We all have a story God is waiting to write in and through us if we can gather the courage to step out of our boat. So, with that in mind, we are ALL John Andrews! Just step out and let God write His story through you!

We would love to hear from you. When you take this next step, we would love to hear your "out of the boat" story. You can visit www.UtterlyAmazed.com and click right on the homepage in order to tell us your story.

Also, if you are looking for a tool to use to help start conversations about Jesus, we have t-shirts available on our website as well.

If you would like for John Andrews to speak to your church, group, or team you can find more information at:

https://www.utterlyamazed.com/speakingrequests

Tell Us Your Story

We hope our stories of how God has worked in and through us has encouraged you. Maybe your story of how God has worked in and through you when you were courageous enough to step out of the boat can inspire someone else. We would love for you to share your story with us, so that we might share it with others and brag on Jesus.

Simply go to https://www.utterlyamazed.com/outsidetheboat and enter your own story of you stepping out on the water with Jesus.

You can also follow us on social media at the following:

Facebook:
Utterly Amazed: Stories from Outside the Boat

Instagram:
@utterlyamazedbook